Mealsfor1–2

50 exciting and tasty recipes

Meals for 1–2

50 exciting and tasty recipes

VINCENT SQUARE BOOKS

First published in Great Britain in 2011 by
Vincent Square Books
an imprint of Kyle Books
www.kylebooks.com

ISBN 978 0 85783 050 0

A Cataloguing in Publication record for this title is
available from the British Library.

10 9 8 7 6 5 4 3 2 1

Text copyright © various, see pp.123–125
Photography © various, see page 126–127
Design © 2011 Kyle Books Limited

Design **Nicky Collings**
Project Editors **Vicky Orchard and Estella Hung**
Production **Nic Jones and David Hearn**

Colour reproduction by Scanhouse in Malaysia
Printed and bound in China by C&C Offset
Printing Co., Ltd

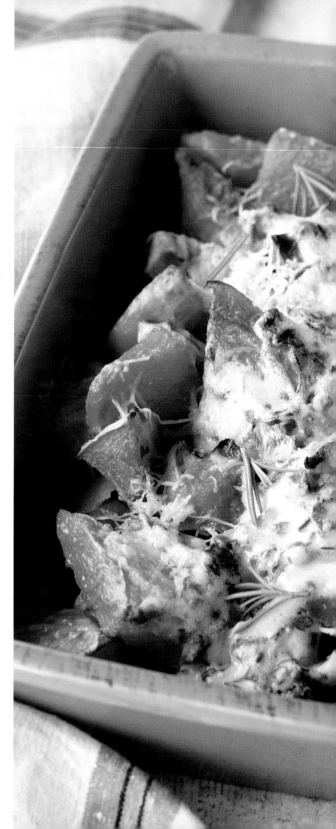

Contents

Introduction

Cooking inspiring and delicious meals for one or two people can be as big a challenge as putting together a feast for large numbers – you want to cook something tasty and satisfying but at the same time ensure you're not left with a glut of leftover ingredients or eating the same meal every day for rest of the week. These recipes are specifically geared to using fewer ingredients and feeding fewer people than the standard four people servings of your average cookbook so that won't happen. There are a huge range of meals to choose from – cooking for smaller numbers doesn't mean you have to sacrifice on taste or just stick to one type of dish – you can cook anything from a summery salad to a light meal, a heartier meat or fish dish or a tasty vegetarian option. There are even gluten-free recipes for coeliacs and vegan ones for those with more specific dietary requirements. Throughout the book these dishes are highlighted with a GF or V symbol in order to make them easy to identify.

Making salads (Chapter 1) is a great way of catering to smaller numbers. Quick to put together if you're just cooking for yourself and want something on the table as soon as possible they are also a nutritious and healthy option. Pear, Pancetta, Toasted Pine Nut & Endive Salad (page 13) is ideal for a night in on your own and if you are super organised you can even prepare

it ahead to take into work for your lunch the following day. Salads are fantastic meals for feeding less people as they combine storecupboard essentials with a few fresh ingredients, helping you cut down on shopping time hunting down specific foods. Feta & Chickpea Salad with Peppers & Coriander (page 14) combines canned chickpeas with delicious fresh vegetables and feta to make a satisfying salad – and you can substitute the chickpeas for cannellini or borlotti beans, so adapting the recipe to the contents of your cupboards.

Cooking lighter dishes (Chapter 2) can be an ideal means of feeding a smaller number of mouths as they tend to require fewer ingredients and you

can usually finish them off between two people so you're not left with plates of leftovers or the prospect of eating the same meal again the next day. Smoked Ham & Mushroom Risotto (page 24) is an easy supper for two people and a versatile dish to have in your repertoire as it can be adapted to use up any spare vegetables that you already have. Rice is a useful storecupboard staple and a great base for a wide variety of dishes – Bacon & Egg-fried Rice (page 32) is a quick and simple meal that is also a clever way of using up any leftover cooked rice from your fridge. Eggs are a particularly handy ingredient to make meals for one or two as they can form the base of omelettes, frittatas or tortillas, where the ingredients can be easily measured to create a meal for one or two diners. Spicy Indian Omelette (page 35) is a mouthwatering dish requiring few ingredients and can even be used in sandwiches for lunch or a snack if you're not eating it all immediately. Like rice, pasta is a good base for lots of different dishes and if you have a packet in the cupboard then you only need to add a few fresh ingredients from your fridge, or those purchased from a quick supermarket shop, to create delicious dishes. Fusillii Tricolore with Lemon & Fennel (page 43) is a simple but satisfying meal made from only a small list of ingredients as is Pappardelle with Pancetta & Cavolo Nero (page 27). Pasta dishes are another easily adaptable meal – the pappardelle works equally well with green cabbage and bacon – and so a fantastic way of using what ingredients you already have and limiting the amount of food that goes to waste because it goes off before you can use it all up.

Just because you're cooking for yourself, or for yourself and plus one, doesn't mean that you have to skimp on interesting ingredients or steer clear of heartier meals. Certain cuts of meat lend themselves to cooking for smaller numbers as a chop, steak or chicken breast comes as a perfect portion size. Caramelised Chicken (page 48) combines basic dried spices and herbs such as thyme and chilli flakes with soy sauce and tomato ketchup to caramelise chicken legs and when you've made the

recipe once you can adjust the balance of ingredients to your own tastebuds as well as to the ingredients you have to hand. Pan-fried Pork with Beans (page 51) uses pork loin steaks for a winter warmer for two, and the accompanying beans can be those of your choice, while Pigeon with Pomegranate Sauce (page 55) and Duck Breast with Spiced Lentils & Caramelised Apples (page 61) are more unusual options, ideal for a special occasion. You can even adapt classic recipes for fewer diners by making individual portions instead one big dish – Beef Wellington with Mushroom & Mustard Sauce (page 65) sees this traditional recipe made into a pastry each.

Like certain cuts of meat, some fish are a great ingredient for feeding one or two as they are ideally sized for a single serving. Mackerel are perfect for smaller numbers – try Grilled Mackerel with Gooseberries & Elderflower (page 76) or Pan-fried Mackerel with Fennel, Grapefruit, Caper & Parsley Salad (page 80). Seafood is also easy to scale for one or two, ensuring little is left over or goes to waste, and provides a tasty addition to pasta – Pasta with Clams (page 88) – or rice dishes such as Quick Crab & Mushroom Kedgeree (page 95).

Cooking vegetarian meals (Chapter 5) works well for one or two as ingredients can often be substituted and they are a great way of using up vegetables that you have left over from making other recipes. Five-A-Day Mixed Vegetable Stir-fry (page 107) can be made from the contents of your fridge and Southern Vegetable Curry (page 111) is quick and easy to make, with a short list of ingredients. Capri Lemon Pasta with Peas, Broad Beans & Asparagus (page 112) can be made with fresh or frozen peas and beans, allowing you to utilise the contents of your freezer.

Salads

Pear, Pancetta, Toasted Pinenut & Endive Salad

All too often you make a yummy, healthy salad option only to find, come lunchtime, it's turned soggy and unappetising. This one's great – it's substantial and won't spoil easily. Red endive is a delicious ingredient: a cross between Belgian endive and radicchio de Treviso. Keep the dressing separate until you are ready to eat it – that way you're guaranteed a crispy salad.

 1 Serving   **GF** Gluten-free

1 unpeeled pear, cored
1 head red endive, end
   removed
a handful of pinenuts,
   toasted
100g smoked pancetta, diced
half a handful of chervil,
   chopped
fennel tops (fronds),
   chopped

For the dressing:
2 tablespoons sherry vinegar
1 tablespoon honey
1 teaspoon wholegrain
   mustard
3 tablespoons extra virgin
   olive oil
pinch of salt

Cut the pear into 8 pieces. Don't be tempted to make the pieces smaller, otherwise they will bruise and taste horrible.

Peel the leaves apart on the endive and mix with the pear.

Toast the pinenuts in a dry frying pan. Remove them from the pan as soon as you can smell them toasting. Throw in the pancetta and allow to bubble and crisp for a few minutes. Remove, leave to cool and then add to the salad, along with the roughly chopped chervil and fennel fronds.

For the dressing, simple combine all the ingredients. Don't add too much salt because there's already a lot in the pancetta. Pour into a jar.

Seal the dressing and salad separately, throw into your bag and try to resist until lunchtime.

Feta & Chickpea Salad with Peppers & Coriander

For speed this recipe uses ready-grilled peppers, but if you can't find any, you can substitute 4 medium tomatoes, cubed – although peppers taste better. You can also make this with cannellini or borlotti beans if you are not a fan of chickpeas.

2 Servings **GF** Gluten-free

200g green beans
2 large red peppers,
   ready grilled, peeled, and
   deseeded
2 heaped tablespoons mint
   or coriander leaves
1 large garlic clove
100ml extra virgin olive oil
3 tablespoons lemon juice or
   red wine vinegar
sea salt and freshly ground
   pepper
400g canned chickpeas,
   rinsed well and drained
4 large handfuls of rocket or
   other green salad
150g feta cheese
12 black olives

Bring a saucepan of water to the boil while you trim and slice the green beans. Blanch the beans, then set aside to drain.

Cut the peppers into long thin strips and chop any large mint leaves. Smash the garlic with salt.

Make a salad dressing with the garlic, olive oil, lemon juice, salt and pepper. Mix half the dressing with the chickpeas, add half the mint and leave to marinate until ready to serve.

Mix the rocket and green beans with the remaining salad dressing. Place the rocket and green beans on individual plates or a serving dish. Scatter over the chickpeas, then place the strips of pepper on top, then crumble with the feta cheese. Sprinkle over the olives and remaining mint.

Serve immediately with warm Middle Eastern flatbread.

Cos Lettuce, Tuna, Quail's Eggs & Roasted Plum Tomatoes

• •

The cooking of the tuna for this salad can be done in advance, and if you have always found tinned tuna dry and tasteless, cooking the fish in this way will make you think again!

 2 Servings   **GF** Gluten-free

4 x 100g tuna steaks
3 garlic cloves, chopped
1 sprig fresh rosemary
1 stick lemongrass, split in two
1 small red chilli, deseeded and chopped (optional)
300ml olive oil
12 quail's eggs
4 firm plum tomatoes, halved
3 tablespoons extra virgin olive oil
salt and freshly ground black pepper
3 tablespoons mayonnaise
1 tablespoon balsamic vinegar
juice of 1 lemon
1 tablespoon flatleaf parsley, finely chopped
1 small head of cos lettuce, cut into strips
3 spring onions, thinly sliced
2 lemons, halved, to serve

Preheat the oven to 230°C/450°F/gas mark 8. First cook the tuna. Place the steaks in a heavy-based frying pan with the garlic, rosemary, lemon grass and chilli (if using), and pour over the olive oil. Bring to simmering point over a low heat and cook for about 10 minutes. Remove from the heat and leave to cool in the oil.

Meanwhile, cook the quail's eggs. Place them in a pan of cold water, bring to the boil and cook for 1 minute. Drain immediately. Peel the eggs under cold running water, cut in half and set aside.

Place the tomatoes in a roasting pan, sprinkle with 1 tablespoon of the extra virgin olive oil, salt and pepper and bake for 5–8 minutes. Remove from the oven and keep warm.

Make the dressing: mix the mayonnaise, vinegar, the remaining olive oil, lemon juice and parsley together in a bowl. Whisk well with a fork and season.

Toss the cos lettuce, spring onions and quail's eggs in the dressing. Add the roasted plum tomatoes and crumble the tuna over the top. Serve with the lemon halves, accompanied by warm pitta bread.

Chickpea, Salt Cod, Roasted Red Onion & Parsley Salad

You can find pre-soaked salt cod in some delicatessens, otherwise ask your fishmonger or make enquiries at the fish counter at the supermarket.

2 Servings **GF** Gluten-free

4 small red onions

3–4 tablespoons extra-virgin olive oil

salt and freshly ground black pepper

300ml milk

300ml water

2 bay leaves

450g salt cod, pre-soaked overnight

1½ tablespoons sherry vinegar

1 garlic clove, finely chopped

1 teaspoon French mustard

1 tablespoon flatleaf parsley

400g cooked chickpeas

Preheat the oven to 200°C/400°F/gas mark 6. Place the onions in a roasting pan with a little oil and seasoning. Bake for 20 minutes. Remove from the oven and leave to cool slightly, then cut into segments. While the onions are cooking, place the milk and water in a large saucepan with the bay leaves and bring to the boil. Add the well-drained salt cod and simmer for about 10–15 minutes, skimming the cooking liquor when necessary. Drain the salt cod well when cooked.

Meanwhile, make the dressing: mix together the oil, vinegar, garlic, mustard and half the parsley. Whisk well with a fork and season with plenty of freshly ground black pepper. Toss the chickpeas, onions, and warm cod in the dressing. Serve sprinkled with the remaining parsley. If served as a main course, accompany with roast or baked potatoes.

Warm Smoked Chicken, Red Onion & Spinach Salad

You could also try this salad substituting the chicken with smoked quail, smoked mackerel or, even better, smoked eel.

 2 Servings **GF** Gluten-free

1 medium red onion, sliced

1 tablespoon soft brown sugar

3 tablespoons balsamic vinegar

3 tablespoons red wine vinegar

salt and freshly ground black pepper

1 teaspoon French mustard

2 tablespoons extra virgin olive oil

3 tablespoons olive oil

300g baby spinach leaves

600g smoked chicken, boned and roughly chopped

1 punnet of mustard and cress

To marinate the onion, mix together the sugar, 1 tablespoon of the balsamic vinegar, the wine vinegar and a pinch of salt in a bowl. Stir until the salt and sugar have dissolved, then add the onion. Toss well and leave to marinate for at least 20 minutes.

To make the dressing, mix together the mustard and the remaining balsamic vinegar in a bowl until well blended, then add the oils, whisking thoroughly with a fork or whisk. Season. Dress the spinach with a couple of tablespoons of the dressing and toss well.

Place the chicken, the drained marinated onion and the remaining dressing in a frying pan and heat gently over a low flame, stirring frequently. When the dressing starts to simmer, remove from the heat. Spoon out on to the dressed spinach, sprinkle with the cress and serve. Boiled new potatoes would be a perfect accompaniment.

Light Meals

Smoked Ham & Mushroom Risotto

An easy supper that you can adapt to use up any spare veg – the trick is just to keep stirring!

2 Servings   **GF**   Gluten-free

12g butter
½ tablespoon oil
½ onion, finely chopped
125g Arborio rice
225ml fresh vegetable stock
150ml dry white wine
75g button mushrooms, wiped and sliced
1 red pepper, deseeded and finely sliced
65g smoked ham, finely sliced
1 tablespoon lemon juice
1 tablespoon single cream
salt and freshly ground black pepper

Melt the butter and oil in a large frying pan. Gently fry the onion for 2–3 minutes until it starts to soften. Stir in the rice, making sure it is well coated with the butter and oil, and cook for 1 minute.

Add the stock and wine gradually, allowing the rice to soak up each addition before adding more. Continue to stir and add the stock until the rice is cooked. This will take about 20–25 minutes. Add the mushrooms, pepper, ham, lemon juice and cream, and season to taste.

Cook for 1–2 minutes, then serve immediately.

Variations: Replace the red pepper with blanched asparagus tips, or add a handful of frozen peas or sweetcorn – whatever takes your fancy!

Replace the cream with low-fat crème fraîche for a lower-fat alternative.

Pappardelle with Pancetta & Cavolo Nero

Cavolo nero is a curly black cabbage that dates back to Roman times. Crinkly green cabbage works just as well. Pancetta cubetti are small chunks of sweet, Italian bacon. Alternatively, use cubes of thick-cut streaky bacon.

 2 Servings

125g pappardelle
1 tablespoon olive oil
125g pancetta cubetti
2 cloves garlic, finely
   chopped
100g cavolo nero, stalks
   removed and roughly
   chopped
salt and freshly ground black
   pepper
75ml white wine
2 tablespoons double cream,
   crème fraîche or half-fat
   crème fraîche
2 tablespoons freshly grated
   Parmesan

Heat a large saucepan of salted water and bring to the boil. Add the pasta and cook for 6–8 minutes, until al dente (still retains a 'bite').

Meanwhile, heat the oil in a medium saucepan and when hot add the pancetta and garlic. Cook for 2–3 minutes until the pancetta is slightly crisp.

Add the cavolo nero and stir to wilt in the oil. Season wth salt and freshly ground black pepper. Add the wine and boil for 2–3 minutes until reduced. Add the cream and Parmesan and heat through. Drain the pasta, stir into the sauce and serve immediately.

Rosemary Porcini

Porcini is the god of all mushrooms. Their season is summer to autumn and, although they are good dried, there is nothing quite like fresh ones. If you can't get hold of porcini, use an interesting mix of farmed or wild mushrooms. Serve with White Bean Truffle Purée and griddled bread.

2 Servings **GF** Gluten-free **V** Vegan

300g porcini or mixed mushrooms

1½ tablespoons extra virgin olive oil

½ garlic clove, finely chopped

1 sprig of rosemary, picked and finely chopped

2 sage leaves, finely chopped

sea salt and ground black pepper

½ tablespoon red wine vinegar, preferably Cabernet Sauvignon

For the White Bean Truffle Purée:

1 tablespoon extra virgin olive oil

½ shallot, finely chopped

1 garlic clove, finely chopped

3 sprigs of thyme, stalks discarded

½ x 300g can cannellini beans

2 tablespoons truffle oil

salt and pepper

Wipe the mushrooms clean with a damp cloth and cut into rough 0.5cm slices. (Try to keep the slices a similar size so that they will all cook evenly.)

Heat half the oil in a large frying pan and add half the mushrooms, or just enough to cover the base. (Overcrowding the pan will cause the temperature to drop and the mushrooms will end up steaming rather than frying. That would be sacrilege!) Cook over a high heat for 3 minutes. Toss the pan, add half the garlic and herbs and a good pinch of salt and pepper and cook for a further 2 minutes, until coloured and tender.

Set aside and repeat with the remaining mushrooms, garlic and herbs, finishing this second batch with a dash of red wine vinegar. Mix with the previously cooked mushrooms and serve as suggested above.

To make the White Bean Truffle Purée, heat the olive oil and cook the shallot, garlic and thyme leaves over a medium heat until softened. Drain and rinse the beans, add to the pan and warm through with 25ml water. Transfer to a blender or food processor and pulse, adding the truffle oil to taste. Season with salt and pepper.

Tip: Truffle oil doesn't like heat, so always add it after the ingredients have finished cooking. Also bear in mind that truffle oil goes rancid quite quickly, so if you've had some open for a while, sniff it first to make sure it is still all right.

Hot Chilli Prawns
on Yellow Shi Noodles

The flavours in this recipe are spicy, sweet and delicately tangy. The tomato ketchup creates the sweetness and gives a great colour too. Shi noodles are a great accompaniment. They are wheatflour noodles, thinner than spaghetti and they absorb the flavours of the sauce really well. Do make sure you serve this dish instantly, otherwise the herbs start to wilt!

 2 Servings

150g dried yellow shi noodles or other wheatflour noodles
2 tablespoons olive oil, plus extra for drizzling
6 large garlic cloves, crushed and chopped
1 tablespoon freshly grated ginger
3 medium red chillies, deseeded and chopped
300g fresh raw tiger prawns, shelled and deveined (tail on or off, optional)
100ml boiling water
1 tablespoon lime juice
2 spring onions, chopped lengthways
4 tablespoons freshly chopped coriander, stalks and leaves

For the sauce:
200ml boiling water
5 tablespoons ketchup
2 tablespoons light soy sauce
1 tablespoon soft brown sugar
2 teaspoons cornflour

Prepare the noodles according to the instructions on the packet, drain and immediately refresh under cold running water to rinse away the starch and keep them springy. Set aside.

Mix all the ingredients for the sauce and set aside.

Heat a wok over high heat and add the olive oil. Add the garlic, ginger and chillies, stir-fry for a few seconds then add the prawns and stir-fry until they start to go pink.

Stir in the sauce ingredients and cook for less than 1 minute, then add the 100ml boiling water, the lime juice, spring onions and coriander.

Refresh the prepared noodles under boiling water, then drizzle with some olive oil and divide between 2 bowls. Place the prawns and sauce on top and serve immediately.

Bacon & Egg-fried Rice

This recipe can be made from leftover rice stored in the fridge.

2 Servings

1 tablespoon vegetable oil
2 eggs, beaten
80g unsmoked streaky
  bacon rashers, chopped
  into small dice
70g frozen peas
300g cooked cold rice
2 tablespoons light soy
  sauce
1 tablespoon sesame oil
ground white pepper

Heat a wok over high heat and add the vegetable oil. Tip the beaten eggs into the wok, stir to scramble, then remove and set aside.

Put the bacon into the same wok and stir-fry until browned and slightly crispy.

Throw in the frozen peas and stir-fry for less than a minute. Add the rice and mix well until the rice has broken down.

Add the egg back into the wok and stir through. Season with light soy sauce, sesame oil and a pinch of ground white pepper and serve immediately.

Spicy
Indian Omelette

· ·

Every culture has its own version of an omelette – this one's from Delhi.

1 Serving   **GF** Gluten-free

2 organic eggs
1 heaped tablespoon finely
  chopped onion
1 heaped tablespoon
  chopped coriander
1 large tomato, finely
  chopped
½ teaspoon freshly roasted
  cumin
salt and freshly ground
  pepper
sunflower oil or clarified
  butter

Heat a frying pan on a high heat. Whisk the eggs in a bowl. Add the remainder of the ingredients, season well with salt and freshly ground pepper. Put a little oil into the pan – it should be very hot. Pour in the egg mixture. It will start to cook immediately so quickly pull the edges of the omelette towards the centre with a plastic or metal slice, tilting the pan so that the uncooked egg runs to the sides. Continue to tilt the pan until most of the egg is set and will not run any more. The omelette may need to cook for a further 5 seconds to brown the bottom. The centre should still be soft and moist.

To fold the omelette flip the edge below the handle of the pan into the centre, then hold the plate so that the omelette will flip over again, then half roll, half slide the omelette on to the plate so that it lands folded into three. It should take no more than 30 seconds in all to make the omelette.

Serve immediately or use in sandwiches.

Cheat's Margherita Pizza

An old favourite on the table in minutes.

2 Servings

4 tablespoons tomato pizza
  topping
1 thin and crispy pizza base
50g mozzarella, grated
1 plum tomato, sliced
4 basil leaves, torn
pinch of oregano

Preheat the oven to 220°C/425°F/gas mark 7.

Spread the topping over the pizza base. Sprinkle the mozzarella evenly over the topping. Arrange the sliced tomatoes on top and sprinkle over the basil leaves and oregano.

Bake for 10–12 minutes or until golden and crisp.

Pizza with Caramelised Onions, Blue Cheese & Rosemary

A pizza is a perfect meal for two – easily divisible into an even number of slices each. This one is a classic combination of cheese and onion.

 Servings

200g pizza dough
  recipe (see below)
2–3 tablespoons olive oil
4 onions, thinly sliced
semolina, if using pizza
  paddle
50g Gorgonzola or Cashel
  Blue cheese
1 teaspoon finely chopped
  fresh rosemary

First make the caramelised onions because they take a long time to cook. (They are so delicious with steaks or even on toast that it's worth cooking 2–3 times the recipe and keeping them in the fridge.) Heat the olive oil in a heavy saucepan, toss in the onions and cook over a low heat for whatever length of time it takes for them to soften and caramelise to a golden brown – about 30–45 minutes.

Preheat the oven to 240°C/475°F/gas mark 9. Roll out the dough as thinly as possible into a round 25–30cm in diameter.

Sprinkle some semolina on to the pizza paddle and place the dough on top. Cover the surface of the dough to within 2cm of the edge with caramelised onions. Crumble the blue cheese and scatter over the top, then sprinkle with chopped rosemary. Drizzle with a little olive oil and slide off the paddle into the fully preheated oven.

Bake for 10–12 minutes and serve immediately.

Pizza Dough

The basic white yeast bread dough is multi-purpose. It takes about 5 hours from start to finish, but for much of that time the bread is rising or baking so it's not 'your time'. In reality, the time spent kneading and making is about 20 minutes. Once you've made it, shape it in loaves or use it for plaits, rolls, twists or for pizza bases.

Makes 1 pizza

3g yeast
70ml water, more as needed
$\frac{1}{3}$ tablespoon olive oil
$\frac{2}{3}$ teaspoon salt
1.6g sugar
8g rye flour

Preheat the oven to 230°C/450°F/gas mark 8.

Mix the yeast with 25ml lukewarm water until dissolved. Put the olive oil, salt and sugar into a bowl with 25ml very hot water, stir until the sugar and salt are dissolved. Add 25ml cold water. By now, the liquid should be lukewarm or blood temperature, so combine with the yeast.

Sift the flour into a bowl, make a well in the centre and pour in most of the lukewarm liquid. Mix to a loose dough adding the remainder of the liquid, or more flour or liquid if necessary. Turn the dough on to a floured board, cover and leave to relax for approx. 5 minutes. Then knead for about 10 minutes or until smooth, springy and elastic (if kneading in a food mixer with a dough hook, 5 minutes is usually long enough).

Put the dough in a bowl. Cover the top tightly with clingfilm – yeast dough rises best in a warm, moist atmosphere. If you want to speed up the rising process put the bowl near your cooker, or a radiator, or close to an Aga. Rising time depends on the temperature; however, the bread will taste better if it rises more slowly. When the dough has more than doubled in size, knead again for about 2–3 minutes or until all the air has been forced out – this is called 'knocking back'. Leave to relax again for 10 minutes.

Roll the dough out as thinly as possible into rounds 25–30cm in diameter or your chosen size. Spare dough can be shaped into rolls, loaves and plaits. Sprinkle some semolina on to a pizza paddle and place the dough on top. Cover with your chosen topping and bake for 10–12 minutes.

Pizza with Broccoli, Mozzarella & Garlic Slivers

This simple, yet slightly unusual pizza is easy to make and requires only a few ingredients, but lacks nothing in terms of flavour.

 Servings

200g pizza dough
   recipe (page 38)
110g calabrese or
   green broccoli
semolina, if using pizza
   paddle
2 tablespoons olive oil
2–3 garlic cloves, cut into
   thin slivers
75g mozzarella, grated
10g Parmigiano Reggiano,
   grated (optional)
sea salt

Preheat the oven to 230°C/450°F/gas mark 8.

Cook the broccoli florets in boiling salted water until al dente.

Roll out the dough as thinly as possible into a round 25–30cm in diameter. Sprinkle some semolina on to the pizza paddle and place the dough on top. Brush the surface of the dough with olive oil. Sprinkle on the slivers of garlic, arrange the broccoli on top and sprinkle with mozzarella and a little Parmesan if liked. Drizzle with olive oil and season with sea salt. Slide off the paddle onto a hot baking sheet.

Bake for 10–12 minutes and serve immediately.

Fusilli Tricolore with Lemon & Fennel

The sharp citrus tang of lemon cuts through the sweet aniseed flavour of fennel to get your taste buds really tingling.

 2 Servings

250g fusilli tricolore
1 bulb fennel, roughly
    chopped
2 cloves garlic, chopped
2 tablespoons olive oil
150ml white wine
zest and juice of 1 lemon
salt and freshly ground black
    pepper
20g flatleaf parsley, chopped
Parmesan, freshly grated, to
    serve

Cook the pasta in a large pan of boiling water following the instructions on the packet.

Meanwhile, place the fennel, garlic and olive oil in a saucepan and cook with the lid on over a moderate heat for 10–15 minutes until soft. Add the wine, lemon juice and seasoning and cook for a further 1–2 minutes. Add the zest of the lemon.

Drain the pasta, reserving a little of the water to combine with the sauce. Add the sauce to the pasta and finish with the parsley.

Serve immediately with freshly grated Parmesan.

Bacon & Cabbage with Crispy Onions

A good accompaniment to pork, but just as delicious eaten for lunch with warm crusty bread.

 2 Servings **GF** Gluten-free

25g butter
1 tablespoon oil
4 rashers rindless smoked
   streaky bacon, cut into
   pieces
150g spring greens
1 tablespoon crispy onion
   topping

Heat the butter and oil in a large frying pan or wok, add the bacon and stir-fry for 3–4 minutes.

Add the spring greens and stir-fry for a further 2–3 minutes. Sprinkle over the crispy onion topping and serve.

Variation: Replace the crispy onion topping with croûtons or toasted breadcrumbs.

Meat Dishes

Caramelised Chicken

This is the perfect midweek supper. It's tasty, cheap and quick to prepare. Everyone will love it and when you've made it once you can become as experimental with it as you like. This is a recipe that will be in your repertoire for years to come.

 2 Servings

For the marinade:
½ teaspoon dried thyme
1 tablespoon dark soft
  brown sugar
1½ tablespoons
  Worcestershire sauce
¼ teaspoon chilli flakes or
  chilli paste
1 tablespoon balsamic
  vinegar
1 tablespoon dark soy
  sauce
1 tablespoon tomato
  ketchup
1½ tablespoons olive oil

For the chicken:
2 chicken legs
2 large red onions, peeled
  and cut into wedges
5 cherry tomatoes on the
  vine
2 large baking potatoes,
  to serve

Preheat the oven to 200°C/400°F/gas mark 6. Put all the marinade ingredients in a big sandwich bag, add the chicken and the onion wedges. Shake around so all the ingredients get well coated in the marinade.

When you are ready to cook, put the chicken legs into a roasting dish with the marinade, onions and the tomatoes. Cook in the oven for 15–20 minutes until the chicken is cooked through. The tomatoes should burst and the onions will go crispy around the edges. Meanwhile, cook the potatoes in the microwave at 800W for 8 minutes – you can pop them in the oven with the chicken when they are done to crisp up the skins.

To serve, put the potatoes on plates and add the chicken, roast tomatoes and onion together with the marinade.

Pan-fried Pork with Beans

A great winter warmer. Serve with plenty of bread to soak up the juices. If you prefer, replace the cannellini beans with kidney beans or mixed beans.

2 Servings

2½ tablespoons olive oil
50g shallots, peeled and finely chopped
2 pork loin steaks
1½ x 410g cans cannellini beans, drained
½ chicken stock cube, made up with 300ml boiling water
10g flatleaf parsley, finely chopped
10g mint, torn into pieces
1 ciabatta loaf
60g herb salad

Heat 1 tablespoon of the olive oil in a large frying pan over a medium heat and fry the shallots gently until softened. Add the pork loin steaks and brown on both sides.

Add the cannellini beans and stock, cover and simmer for 15–20 minutes. Remove the lid, and add the remaining olive oil, the parsley and mint. Serve with ciabatta and crisp green salad.

Sichuan Pepper Beef with Five-a-day Vegetables & Five-spice Gravy

Chinese five-spice is the key to this recipe as it flavours the gravy beautifully. This is a really balanced meal of protein and vegetables.

2 Servings

2 sirloin steaks, cut into
  strips
2 tablespoons groundnut oil
1 medium red chilli,
  deseeded and chopped
½ onion, chopped
1 small handful broccoli
1 small handful chopped
  mangetout
1 small handful chopped
  carrots
1 small handful chopped
  baby corn
300ml hot fresh beef or
  vegetable stock
1 tablespoon light soy sauce
1 tablespoon cornflour
  blended with 2 tablespoons
  cold water
1 spring onion, finely sliced
salt and ground white pepper

For the marinade:
1 tablespoon shaoxing rice
  wine or dry sherry
2 teaspoons ground Sichuan
  pepper
1 teaspoon dark soy sauce
½ teaspoon Chinese
  five-spice powder
2 garlic cloves, crushed and
  finely chopped

For the jasmine rice:
175g jasmine rice, washed
  until the water runs clear
300ml boiling water

Mix all the marinade ingredients in a bowl and marinate the beef for as long as possible, overnight is best.

Heat a wok over high heat and add the oil. Stir-fry the marinated beef for 2 minutes.

Add the red chilli and onion and stir-fry for less than 1 minute then add the rest of the vegetables and stir-fry for 1 minute.

Add the stock (it needs to be hot) and mix well. Season with light soy sauce. Bring to the boil, add the blended cornflour and stir well.

Add the spring onion, season to taste and serve with jasmine rice.

To make the jasmine rice, place the rice in a heavy-based saucepan and add the boiled water. Bring to the boil then cover with a tight-fitting lid and reduce to a low heat. Cook for 15–20 minutes. Uncover the pan and remove from the heat. Fluff up the rice grains with a fork and serve immediately.

Pigeon with Pomegranate Sauce

This is a Syrian dish based on the same concept as the French duck with orange. The pomegranate syrup, which is quite sharp, works in the same way as orange juice, cutting the richness of the game. You'll find pomegranate syrup in most Middle Eastern stores or supermarkets that stock more unusual ingredients.

 2 Servings **GF** Gluten-free

2 pigeons
2 tablespoons extra virgin olive oil
1 small red onion
50g walnut pieces (or halves broken into pieces)
2 tablespoons pomegranate syrup
4 tablespoons water
2 heaped teaspoons sugar
sea salt and freshly ground black pepper

Preheat the oven to 180°C/350°F/gas mark 4. The easiest way to cook this dish is in an ovenproof frying pan or sauté pan. Alternatively preheat a small roasting pan or gratin dish into which the pigeons fit snugly.

First spatchcock the birds. You have to remove the backbone first. Place one pigeon, breast-side down, on a board. Insert a pair of sharp scissors down the backbone, working from the leg end towards the neck. Cut along both sides of the backbone – it will come out as a long thin rectangle. Turn the pigeon over and press down so that it sits as flat as possible. Do the same with the second bird.

Heat a lidded frying pan to medium-hot, add the olive oil and brown the pigeons on all sides. Remove the birds and set aside.

While the pigeons are browning, quarter the onion then slice. Add the onion to the pan with the walnuts. Turn the heat to low, cover with a lid and gently cook for 5 minutes, until the onion is soft. Pour over the pomegranate syrup and the water, add the sugar and stir to dissolve the sugar into the juices. Season with salt and pepper and return the pigeons to the pan. Turn the pigeons on their breasts to coat in the juices.

Place the pan in the oven, or transfer everything to the prehated ovenproof dish and cook in the oven for 10 minutes if you like your meat on the pink side, or cook for a further 5 minutes if you prefer.

Check after 10 minutes and add a little more water if the juices have reduced too much.

Burmese-style Beef Curry with Vermicelli Rice Noodles

A delicious Burmese curry that you can adapt to your taste. If you cannot take chillies, reduce the quantity given or, if you love spiciness, increase their number; you can also add some crushed dried chillies. This recipe can be served with steamed rice or Chinese vermicelli rice noodles.

 2 Servings

2 tablespoons groundnut oil
2 shallots, peeled and
  chopped
1 tablespoon shrimp paste
350g sirloin steak, cubed
300ml coconut milk
1 lemongrass stalk, chopped
½ teaspoon soft brown sugar
1 tablespoon ground
  coriander seeds
2 tablespoons fish sauce
  (nam pla)
1 handful chopped fresh
  coriander
1 handful chopped Thai basil
  leaves
160g vermicelli rice noodles

For the paste:
4 garlic cloves, crushed and
  finely shopped
1 tablespoon freshly grated
  ginger
2 red chillies, deseeded and
  chopped
1 large onion, peeled and
  chopped
1 teaspoon turmeric

Blend all the paste ingredients together.

Heat a wok over a high heat, add the oil and stir-fry the shallots with the shrimp paste for less than one minute. Add the paste ingredients and stir fry for 1 minute. Add the steak and stir-fry for 2 minutes until browned on all sides.

Stir in the coconut milk. (For a thinner sauce, you could add a little chicken stock at this stage. For a creamier curry you could add some coconut cream.) Add the lemongrass, the brown sugar, ground coriander and fish sauce. Bring to the boil and sprinkle with a handful of chopped fresh coriander and Thai basil leaves.

Bring a large pan of water to the boil and cook the vermicelli rice noodles according to the packet instructions, drain and place in 2 serving bowls. Ladle the curry over the noodles and serve immediately.

Lamb Kebabs with Tzatziki

Tzatziki is a Greek speciality and is a delicious cucumber and yogurt mixture which can be served as part of a mezze, as an accompanying salad or as a sauce to serve with grilled fish or meat.

 8 Servings **GF** Gluten-free

250g lean shoulder or leg of
 lamb

Marinade 1:
75ml natural yogurt
pinch of ground coriander
pinch of ground cumin
pinch of freshly ground
 pepper
squeeze of lemon juice

Marinade 2:
1½ tablespoons extra virgin
 olive oil
good squeeze of lemon juice
1 teaspoon annual marjoram,
 rosemary or thyme leaves
1 garlic clove, crushed
salt and freshly ground black
 pepper

For the Tzatziki;
½ crisp cucumber, peeled
 and diced into 3–5mm dice
Salt
1 garlic clove, crushed
small dash of white wine
 vinegar or lemon juice
215ml Greek yogurt or
 best-quality natural yogurt
2 tablespoons cream
 (optional)
1 level tablespoon freshly
 chopped mint
sugar, salt and freshly
 ground pepper

Kebabs are best barbecued but may also be pan-grilled or cooked under a salamander. Choose kebab skewers carefully. They need to be flat and at least 3mm wide, better still 5mm. If they are round, the meat will swivel as you try to turn it.

Make both marinades. Cut the meat into 2.5cm cubes, season with salt and pepper and put each cube into the one of the marinades for 1 hour at least. Drain the meat and thread on to metal skewers or kebab sticks. Grill for 7–10 minutes over a barbecue, turning and basting with the marinade 2 or 3 times.

Now make the Tzatziki. Put the cucumber dice into a sieve, sprinkle with salt and allow to drain for about 30 minutes. Dry the cucumber on kitchen paper, put into a bowl and mix with the garlic, vinegar or lemon juice, yogurt and cream. Stir in the mint and taste. It may need seasoning with salt, pepper and a little sugar.

Serve with a green salad.

Duck Breast with Spiced Lentils & Caramelised Apples

A delicious treat for two – perfect for a special occasion.

 2 Servings   **GF** Gluten-free

2 duck breasts
salt and freshly ground
    pepper

Puy lentils:
110g Puy lentils
½ carrot
½ onion, stuck with 2 cloves
1 small bouquet garni
juice of freshly squeezed
    lemon, to taste
 butter or extra virgin olive oil
a small handful of freshly
    chopped herbs (e.g. fresh
    oregano, annual marjoram
    or parsley)
sea salt and freshly ground
    pepper

Caramelised apples:
1 eating apple (Cox's Orange
    Pippin or Golden Delicious)
1 teaspoon butter
 ½ tablespoon sugar
squeeze of lemon juice
½ tablespoon Calvados
    (optional)
sprigs of coriander or
    flatleaf parsley, for garnish

1 chilli, finely chopped
1 tablespoons fresh
    coriander
lemon juice, freshly
    squeezed
extra virgin olive oil

Season the duck breasts and score the fat with a sharp knife. Heat a pan-grill over a high heat; cook the duck fat-side down for 15–20 minutes, depending on thickness. Turn over and continue until fully cooked but still tender and juicy. Reduce the heat and cook on a low heat for 10–15 minutes until the fat is crisp and fully cooked. A lot of fat will run out and you may need to pour some off.

Wash the lentils and put them into a large saucepan. Fill with cold water, add the carrot, onion and bouquet garni (see tip below), bring slowly to the boil, reduce the heat and simmer very gently for 10–15 minutes, testing regularly. The lentils should be 'al dente' but not hard. Drain, remove and discard the carrot, onion and bouquet garni. Grease the lentils while warm with a good knob of butter or some extra virgin olive oil, then add lots of freshly squeezed lemon juice and some finely chopped herbs. Season with sea salt and freshly ground pepper. Set aside.

To prepare the apples, peel, core and cut into 5mm slices. Melt the butter in a non-stick frying pan, toss in the apple and cook gently for 5 minutes. Add the sugar and allow to caramelise slightly. Add the lemon juice and Calvados.

Allow it to become syrupy, then remove from the pan and keep warm.

Heat the lentils and stir in the chilli, coriander, and a squeeze of lemon juice. Season with salt and pepper and some olive oil to taste. Divide the lentils between hot plates, arrange a crispy duck breast on top and garnish with apple, sprigs of coriander or flatleaf parsley.

Tip: Bouquet garni is a small bunch of fresh herbs used to flavour stews, casseroles, stocks or soups, usually consisting of parsley stalks, a sprig of thyme, perhaps a bay leaf and an outside stalk of celery, tied together with a little string.

Pork Tenderloin with Pears & Sweet Sherry

The quality of the sherry really makes this dish. You can also use an even sweeter Spanish dessert wine made from the Pedro Ximenez grape, or Marsala, a dessert wine from Sicily. But sweet sherry can be used in a variety of recipes, so a bottle won't be wasted. Pork tenderloin is the small fillet rather than the larger loin of pork. It cooks quickly and small slices of meat work well as tapas.

 2 Servings

450g pork tenderloin
2 tablespoons extra virgin
  olive oil
1 small red onion
2 garlic cloves
1 pear, not too hard if
  possible
sea salt and freshly ground
  black pepper
100ml sweet oloroso sherry
a few tablespoons chicken
  stock (optional)

Heat a lidded sauté pan to medium-hot. (The trick to pan-frying meat is the temperature of the pan. It should be hot enough to brown and seal the meat, but not so hot that you burn the base of the pan, as the sediment left adds a delicious flavour to the final sauce.)

Trim the tenderloin of any white sinew and cut into 2.5cm slices. Add the oil to the pan and when hot add the pork. Cook the slices, browning on both sides. Remove when the meat is sealed and brown, but if the slices are thicker, reduce the heat a little to cook through.

Meanwhile, chop the onion and slice the garlic.

Remove the meat to a bowl, and add the onion and garlic to the pan. Cover the pan with the lid and gently cook the onion, scraping all the tasty sediment left by the meat (add a dash of water to help remove it before it burns if the pan is too hot).

While the onion is cooking, peel the pear, quarter, decore and cut into 1cm slices. Add the pear and continue to cook for a further 5 minutes, covered. When the onion and pear are soft return the meat to the pan, mixing into the onions and season with salt and pepper.

Increase the heat to medium-hot, add the sherry and cook at a brisk simmer for 2 minutes to amalgamate the flavours. If you like your meat with a bit more sauce you can add a few tablespoons chicken stock or even water when the sauce comes to the boil.

Set aside for a few minutes then serve as a tapas or main course.

Beef Wellington with Mushroom & Mustard Sauce

Perfect for special occasions, these individual beef Wellingtons are simply delicious.

2 Servings

1 tablespoon olive oil
25g butter
2 x 125g pieces fillet
   steak
1 red onion, finely diced
125g button mushrooms,
   diced
2 teaspoons wholegrain
   mustard
2 tablespoons dry sherry
salt and freshly ground black
   pepper
375g ready-to-roll puff
   pastry, defrosted
1 egg, beaten, to glaze
150ml red wine
2 tablespoons single cream

Preheat the oven to 220°C/425°F/gas mark 7.

Heat the oil and butter in a frying pan and quickly seal the steaks on both sides. Remove from the pan and allow to cool.

Add the onion and mushrooms to the pan and cook for 6–8 minutes, stirring occasionally. Stir in the mustard, sherry and seasoning, cook for a further 2 minutes and allow to cool.

On a lightly floured surface, cut the pastry in half and roll out one piece large enough to 'wrap' around one steak. Place a heaped teaspoon of the mushroom mixture in the centre of the pastry, top with the beef and place a further spoonful of the mixture on the beef.

Brush the edges of the pastry with water and with a sharp knife make cuts in from the corners. Wrap the pastry around the meat to seal completely and place seal-side down on a baking tray. Repeat with the other steak.

Make pastry leaves with any remaining pastry and stick on top with a little water.

Brush with beaten egg and bake for 20–25 minutes until risen and golden brown.

To make the sauce, add the wine to the remaining mushroom mixture and reduce slightly. Stir in the cream and serve hot with the beef.

Lamb Cutlets on a Warm Tomato & Artichoke Salad

Choose well-trimmed cutlets with dark red meat, unless you are buying new season lamb.

 2 Servings

6 lamb cutlets
salt and freshly ground black
 pepper
½ tablespoon olive oil
25g unsalted butter
½ sprig of fresh rosemary
2 marinated artichokes, cut
 into segments
½ garlic clove, finely
 chopped
2 plum tomatoes, quartered,
 deseeded and cut into
 segments
75g spinach leaves, roughly
 chopped

Preheat the oven to 220°C/425°F/gas mark 7.

Season the cutlets.

Heat the oil and butter with the rosemary in a large frying pan. When the butter begins to foam, sear the cutlets on both sides. Remove them from the pan with the rosemary and arrange on a baking tray. Cook for 5–6 minutes or longer if you prefer your lamb not quite pink.

Meanwhile, return the frying pan to the heat and bring back to sizzling point. Add the artichokes, garlic and tomatoes and quickly toss in the cooking juices. Add the spinach and warm through, checking the seasoning. Distribute the warm salad on individual serving dishes and arrange the cutlets on top. Serve with baked potatoes or buttered basmati rice. Do not accompany with mint sauce!

Pork Fillets with Bergamot Sauce

A dish to keep dieters happy, since there is no added fat. It tastes clean and refreshing, and cooking the chicken in foil parcels means that all the flavours are retained. Serve it with a little lemon and some fluffy white rice.

 2 Servings **GF** Gluten-free

2 large pork fillets
salt and freshly ground black
 pepper
75g butter
2 shallots, very finely
 chopped
40g flour
4 tablespoons dry white wine
3½ tablespoons chopped
 bergamot leaves
1 tablespoon double cream

Preheat the oven to 200°C/400°F/gas mark 6.

Wash the fillets of pork. Pat dry, season and smear with half the butter. Roast in a shallow greased tin for 25 minutes. Allow to rest for 5 minutes before slicing. Arrange slices in a warmed serving dish.

Prepare this sauce while the fillets are in the oven. Sweat the shallots in half the butter until soft. Stir in the flour and cook for about a minute, stirring all the time. Whisk in the stock. Simmer until it thickens, stirring occasionally. Then slowly add the wine and 3 tablespoons of the chopped bergamot. Simmer for several minutes then season to taste. Remove from heat, stir in the cream, pour over arranged pork slices and garnish with remaining chopped bergamot.

Serve with mashed potatoes, and fresh green vegetables such as broccoli.

Chicken & Winter Tarragon Parcel

Winter tarragon makes a good substitute for French tarragon (*Artemisia dracunculus*), not only in winter, when French tarragon has died back into the ground, but also where it is difficult to grow i.e. in humid climates. The leaves of this tarragon are much stronger and more anise than the French variety, so use with care until you get used to it.

 2 Servings **GF** Gluten-free

2 skinless organic chicken breasts
2 garlic cloves, peeled and sliced
6 x 10cm sprigs of winter tarragon, leaves removed and chopped
30g butter
160ml white wine
extra wide tin foil

Preheat the oven to 220°C/425°F/gas mark 7.

Cut two pieces of tin foil 35cm x 50cm. Place them on top of each other. Then fold in half and seal the two long sides leaving the top open. Place the chicken breasts in the foil bag, with the garlic, chopped tarragon and butter. Check the sides of the bag are well sealed, then pour in the white wine and seal the top. Place this on a baking tray and put in the oven for 25 minutes. Once cooked, place the foil bag on to a plate or serving dish before opening to catch all the juices.

Serve with baked potatoes and a crisp green salad.

Pheasant Braised with Cork Gin

Casserole roasting is a technique worth noting. The bird cooks in the steamy atmosphere of the covered casserole, either on top of the stove or in the oven. This method produces lots of cooking juices, which make a delicious little sauce.

2 Servings **GF** Gluten-free

oval casserole dish about 25cm x 7.5cm with a volume of just over 1 litre

1 small pheasant
salt and freshly ground pepper
2 teaspoons extra virgin olive oil
25g streaky bacon, diced
50ml gin or brandy
2 juniper berries, crushed
150ml white wine
sprigs of parsley

Pluck and eviscerate (gut) the pheasant if necessary. Wash inside and out and pat dry.

Season the pheasant with salt and freshly ground pepper. Heat the oil in an oval casserole just large enough to accommodate the pheasant. Toss in the diced bacon and cook for a few minutes until it begins to crisp, remove the bacon and set aside.

Add the pheasant to the pan, breast side down, and allow to brown. Turn the other way up, return the bacon to the casserole, pour in the gin or brandy and flame or boil for a few minutes.

Add the crushed juniper berries. Cover the casserole and simmer gently for about 40 minutes on the stove or transfer to the oven and cook at 180°C/ 350°F/gas mark 4 for the same length of time. Remove the pheasant to a serving dish and keep warm. Decrease the cooking juices, then add the white wine. Allow the sauce to boil up and reduce until slightly thickened.

Joint the pheasant and arrange on a hot serving plate, spoon the sauce over and garnish with sprigs of parsley.

Fish &
Seafood

Grilled Mackerel with Gooseberries & Elderflower

The combination of gooseberries and elderflowers is, of course, a classic. So too is the pairing of mackerel and gooseberries. Serve with lemon and new potatoes. Pre-salting (see below) makes it firmer and tastier.

2 Servings **GF** Gluten-free

2 whole mackerel
2 tablespoons coarse sea salt
5 large elderflower heads
grated zest and juice of 1 lemon
½ red chilli, seeds removed, chopped
1 fresh garlic clove, chopped
½ teaspoon freshly ground black pepper
butter, for frying

To serve:
Gooseberry Compote with Elderflowers (see below)

Gut the fish, but leave the heads on. Slash each fish three times on both sides with a very sharp knife. Using 1½ tablespoons of the coarse sea salt, rub the fish inside and out, then leave to rest for a couple of hours in a cool place. After that time, clean off the salt under a cold tap, then dry the fish completely with kitchen paper.

Cut the white flowers from the green stems of the elderflower heads and mix with the remaining salt, plus the lemon zest, chilli, garlic and black pepper. Fill the fish with this heady mixture. Either fry the fish in hot butter until nicely browned – 4 minutes on each side for a small mackerel – or grill them on a barbeque. Turn the fish only once, as they are tender-fleshed. Serve with the compote.

Gooseberry Compote with Elderflowers

1kg unripe gooseberries
sugar
10 elderflower heads (optional)
200ml elderflowers, picked off the stalks (optional)

Put the washed gooseberries into a shallow, non-corrosive pan, then cover the bottom of the pan with 2mm of water. Put the lid on and bring to the boil. Let the berries bubble gently until they are punctured and collapse, then add the sugar to taste.

You can serve the compote hot as a sauce or cold as a dessert with cream and sugar on top. The inclusion of the elderflowers is optional, but the combined flavour goes wonderfully with fried fish and crispy pork.

Pan-fried Scallops with Bacon & Sherry Vinegar

Scallops with bacon is a traditional Mediterranean combination and the mixture works really well. The sherry vinegar perfectly cuts the richness of both the scallops and bacon. Scallops should be served rare, so don't be tempted to cook them for long. Serve with salad or sauté potatoes.

 2 Servings   **GF** Gluten-free

8 large scallops
2 tablespoons extra virgin olive oil
75g bacon, or 4 rashers
1 garlic clove, chopped
1 level tablespoon chopped rosemary
sea salt and freshly ground black pepper
2 tablespoons sherry vinegar or dry sherry

Trim the hard white muscle from the side of the scallops and rinse them in cold water, then rinse well and place on kitchen paper. Remove the coral or orange roe if you prefer.

Heat the olive oil in a large frying pan to medium-hot and chop the bacon. Add the bacon to the pan and cook until nearly brown; it will carry on cooking a little, but don't remove it as the fat from the bacon flavours the scallops as they cook. Push the bacon to the side and add the scallops. Cook quickly, increasing the heat if need be, for only 1 minute per side.

Add the garlic and the rosemary when you turn the scallops over. Mix in with the bacon. Season with salt and pepper and when the scallops are browned on both sides, add the sherry vinegar and remove from the heat. Toss the scallops and bacon in the sauce and serve immediately.

Pan-fried Mackerel with Fennel, Grapefruit, Caper & Parsley Salad

This is a great light supper for when you're in a rush or just don't want a lot of fuss. The only cooking involved is the mackerel, and that takes about 5 minutes. This recipe uses caperberries, which have a mellower flavour than pickled capers, but use whichever you prefer. If you buy salted capers, rinse them in cold water first, otherwise they will be far too salty for this dish.

2 Servings   **GF** Gluten-free

4 fillets fresh mackerel
1 large bulb of fennel
1 lemon
1 pink grapefruit
a handful of caperberries
a bunch of flatleaf parsley
a handful of watercress
  (optional)
1 tablespoon olive oil, plus
  extra for drizzling
salt and freshly ground black
  pepper

When you buy the mackerel, ask your fishmonger to remove the bones down the middle of the fillets. This is done by cutting a v-shape on either side of the bones and removing them all in one go. If you're brave, try it yourself.

To make the salad, cut the fennel in half and remove the core by cutting a v-shape on either side and easing it out. (You can eat this but it is a bit tough and can be bitter.) Slice the fennel by turning it flat side down and slicing very thinly downwards. Squeeze half the lemon over the fennel to prevent it from going brown.

Peel the skin from the grapefruit using a sharp, serrated knife, trying to remove all the pith with the skin as you do this. Using your knife, remove each segment of fruit and place it in a large bowl. Squeeze in any juice from the bits you have cut off.

Add the fennel to the grapefruit along with the caperberries. Pick off the leaves from the flatleaf parsley and throw them into the bowl, with the watercress, if using; I find this adds a lovely peppery element.

To cook the mackerel, heat the oil in a large non-stick pan. Season the skin-side of the fillets with salt (Maldon sea salt is best), and place in the pan, skin-side down. Hold them flat in the pan with a fish slice to prevent them curling. Cook on each side for 2 minutes.

Add a final squeeze of lemon and remove from the heat. Place a nice big pile of the salad on to a plate and top with the fish. Sprinkle with salt, pepper and a good drizzle of olive oil.

Curried Fish Balls with Bamboo Shoots

Fish balls are like small round dumplings and are made from fish and flour. They can be bought ready prepared in Chinese stores.

 1 Serving

1 tablespoons oil
1 tablespoons Jungle Curry Paste (see below)
225g fish balls
340ml water
1½ tablespoons fish sauce
3 kaffir lime leaves
75g bamboo shoots
½ tablespoon finely sliced krachai (see right)
10 sweet basil leaves

Heat the oil in a large frying pan, add the curry paste, then add the fish balls quickly and stir-fry for 2 minutes. Add the remaining ingredients in turn, stirring well, then bring to the boil. Ladle into a dish, add the basil leaves and serve.

Krachai (Chinese Key)
This annual has aromatic rhizomes and yellow-brown roots, and is used as a flavouring. It also has a medicinal value as an aid to digestion.

Jungle Curry Paste

Makes roughly 12 tablespoons

10 large dried red chillies
1 teaspoon sea salt
20g shallots, peeled and finely chopped
40g garlic, peeled and finely chopped
2 tablespoons finely chopped galangal
4 lemongrass stalks, finely chopped
2 teaspoons coriander seeds
1 tablespoon shrimp paste

The ingredients for the curry paste should be ground using a pestle and mortar. Start with the hardest ingredients then add the other ingredients one at a time. I usually start with the chillies and sea salt – the coarse salt helps to cut through the chilli skin. As you add each ingredient, check the aroma of the paste to see how the new ingredient is balancing with the previous ones. This will ensure that you don't add too much or too little of any ingredient. You are aiming for a harmonious blend with no one flavour dominating.

Proper Breakfast Kippers

When they are lightly smoked, the kippers can be cooked in a little foaming butter on a frying pan instead.

 2 Servings   **GF** Gluten-free

2 undyed kippers
Maître d'Hôtel Butter (see
  below)

For the garnish:
2 lemon segments
2 sprigs of parsley

Put the kippers head downwards into a deep jug. Cover them with boiling water right up to their tails as though you are making tea. Leave for 2–3 minutes to heat through. Lift them out carefully by the tail and serve immediately on hot plates with a pat of Maître d'Hôtel Butter melting on top. Garnish each with a segment of lemon and a sprig of parsley.

Maître d'Hôtel Butter

This is one of the oldest classic flavoured butters. It is good served with a piece of pan-grilled fish or steak.

 2 Servings

110g butter
2 tablespoons finely chopped
  parsley
a few drops of freshly
  squeezed lemon juice

Cream the butter, then add in the parsley and a few drops of lemon juice at a time. Roll into butter pats or form into a roll and wrap in greaseproof paper or tin foil, screwing each end so that it looks like a cracker.

Refrigerate to harden.

Scallops on Pea Purée

A real treat. The freshest scallops still smell of the sea!

2 Servings   **GF** Gluten-free

½ small onion, chopped
1 teaspoon butter
125g peas
dash of white wine
salt and freshly ground black
   pepper
1 teaspoon chervil
1 teaspoon tarragon
½ tablespoon double cream
6 large scallops
butter for frying
deep-fried shredded leek to
   garnish (optional)

Fry the onion in the butter for 5 minutes until softened but not browned. Add the peas and a dash of white wine and leave to bubble for 5–10 minutes.

Season and stir in the chervil, tarragon and cream. Purée until smooth.

Pan-fry the scallops in butter over a high heat for 1–2 minutes each side. Be careful not to overcook or they will be unpleasantly rubbery in texture.

To serve, place a ring of purée on each plate, top with scallops and garnish with a pile of deep-fried shredded leek.

Pasta
with clams

This is a simple fish pasta, served in coastal towns throughout Italy, made with fresh clams (you'll see it as 'pasta alla vongole' on menus). There's no need to add any extra salt apart from the pasta cooking water – clams are salty enough. You need to assemble your guests before you start to cook this dish because it is at its best eaten straight from the pan. Don't serve with cheese as this pasta contains chilli and fish – it's just not done!

2 Servings

500g clams, cleaned and
  drained
1 large garlic clove
1 small red chilli
1 small bunch flatleaf parsley
150g linguine
40ml dry white vermouth or
  white wine
50ml extra virgin olive oil

Place the clams in a large bowl or sink and cover with cold water and leave to soak. Leave for a few minutes, then remove the clams individually, checking none are full of sand or grit and place in a colander. Drain well.

Finely chop the garlic and chilli, removing the seeds if you prefer less heat, and coarsely chop the parsley. Set aside.

Bring a large saucepan of well-salted water to the boil for the pasta. Heat a high-sided lidded sauté pan, add the vermouth and cover with a lid. Cook for about 1–2 minutes until all the clams have opened. Drain over a bowl to catch the liquid.

Add the oil to the sauté pan and cook the garlic and chilli briefly, then add the parsley and the clam liquid, discarding any sediment. Cook the liquid for a few minutes to concentrate flavours.

Check the pasta is al dente, then drain well and add to the clam liquid. At the last minute, add the clams, mixing the pasta off the heat. Serve immediately, dividing first the pasta between bowls and then the clams for easiest results. Pour any remaining juices over each serving.

Roast Salmon with Watercress Sauce

A peppery watercress sauce cuts through the richness of salmon in a great combination of flavours.

2 Servings **GF** Gluten-free

50ml dry white wine
150ml fish stock
142ml double cream
38g watercress, washed
salt and freshly ground black
    pepper
½ tablespoon vegetable oil
2 x 200g salmon fillets

Preheat the oven to 220°C/425°F/gas mark 7.

Pour the wine and the fish stock into a medium saucepan, bring to the boil and reduce by half. Add the double cream and bring to the boil. Add the watercress and cook for 1–2 minutes, seasoning to taste. Remove from the heat.

Pour into a liquidiser or food processor and blend until smooth. Then return the sauce to a clean saucepan.

To cook the salmon, heat a non-stick frying pan, add the oil and place the salmon skin-side down in the pan for 2 minutes over a medium heat. Transfer the salmon to a baking sheet and place in the oven for 8–10 minutes, until just cooked. Remove from the oven and reheat the sauce.

Serve with the watercress sauce and a tomato and shallot salad.

Roasted John Dory with Roasted Tomato & Olive Salsa

John Dory is also known as St Peter's fish. The 'Fisher of Men' is said to have picked out a specimen from the day's catch to throw back into the sea, leaving the imprints of his thumb on one side of the fish and his forefinger on the other. To this day, the silver-grey fish bears the marks on its skin.

 2 Servings **GF** Gluten-free

1 tablespoon olive oil
12.5g unsalted butter
2 x 170g John Dory fillets
4–6 plum tomatoes, quartered
salt and freshly ground black pepper
1 tablespoon extra virgin olive oil
1 lemon, halved

For the salsa:
75g black olives, pitted, rinsed, drained and chopped
75g green olives, pitted rinsed, drained and chopped
½ garlic clove, finely chopped
½ red onion, finely chopped
1½ tablespoons chopped flatleaf parsley
½ tablespoon balsamic vinegar
1 tablespoon extra virgin olive oil
salt and freshly ground black pepper

Preheat the oven to 220°C/425°F/gas mark 7.

Heat the olive oil and butter in a roasting pan and fry the John Dory fillets, browning them on both sides. Add in the tomatoes, season and bake in a preheated oven for about 8–10 minutes.

Meanwhile, prepare the salsa by mixing together all the ingredients. Serve the fish with the softened tomato quarters, a spoonful of the salsa and a drizzle of extra virgin olive oil, accompanied by lemon halves.

Quick Crab
& Mushroom Kedgeree

Kedgeree is a marvellous dish and a great old English Favourite. This is a twist on the classic recipe – simple and so tasty.

2 Servings   **GF** Gluten-free

3 x 200g sachets microwaveable plain boiled rice

115g butter

225g baby button mushrooms, halved

4 spring onions, chopped

450g fresh white crab meat

4 tablespoons roughly chopped fresh parsley

2 tablespoons vegetable oil

1 egg, beaten

salt and freshly ground black pepper

Warm the rice in the microwave on high for 2 minutes. Heat half the butter in a non-stick wok, then warm the rest in a separate pan. Add the mushrooms to the wok and cook for 2–3 minutes.

Add the spring onions, crab meat and parsley and cook for 2–3 minutes. In a separate non-stick wok, heat the oil. Add the beaten egg and cook over a gentle heat, stirring constantly until the egg is scrambled.

Add the warmed rice to the crab mixture and mix well. Then add the egg to the rice, stir well and season.

Finally, stir in the remaining melted butter and serve.

Baked Red Mullet
with Vine Leaves

This could be described as a quintessential Mediterranean dish. Fish, vine leaves and lemons: bastions of the region, all three in abundance. If you happen to have access to raw vine leaves, that's perfect. This recipe uses easier-to-source vine leaves in brine, which are sold in jars at supermarkets. This dish is perfect cooked over charcoal, if you have time.

 2 Servings   **GF** Gluten-free

2–4 red mullet or 2 x 600g
   sea bream
several sprigs of thyme or
   rosemary
1 lemon
4–6 vine leaves, depending
   on size, fresh or tinned
drizzle of extra virgin olive oil
   for cooking and serving

Ask your fishmonger to descale and gut the fish for you but leave on the heads and tails. Wash them thoroughly, inside and out. If using vine leaves in brine, rinse well. Drain on kitchen paper.

Cover a baking tray with foil, place in the oven and preheat to 200°C/400°F/gas mark 6.

Stuff the cavity of the fish with a sprig of thyme and a slice of lemon. Drizzle no more than 1 teaspoon olive oil over each fish.

Place the vine leaves, with the veins facing down, on a work surface. Place the fish on top (you may need to use 2 or 3 overlapping leaves, depending on their size). It looks attractive if you keep the head and tail showing. Wrap up the fish, glaze with some olive oil and place sealed side down on the preheated baking tray. Top with slices of lemon. Bake for about 10 minutes, depending on the size of the fish.

Transfer to a plate, drizzle with extra virgin olive oil and serve immediately.

Parmesan-crusted Cod with Tomato & Olive Dressing

Crunchy-topped fish is complemented by a flavour-packed dressing for a light and delicious main course.

2 Servings

40g fresh white breadcrumbs
25g Parmesan, freshly grated
10g flatleaf parsley, chopped
2 cod fillets, or other firm-fleshed fish, such as cod
½ tablespoon olive oil
salt and freshly ground black pepper

For the dressing:
2 plum tomatoes, skin and seeds removed, chopped
25g Kalamata olives, pitted and chopped
1 tablespoon olive oil
10g basil leaves, torn
salt and freshly ground black pepper

Preheat the oven to 190°C/375°F/gas mark 5.

Mix together the breadcrumbs, Parmesan and parsley, and season to taste.

Brush the cod fillets with the olive oil and coat with the breadcrumb mixture. Place on a baking sheet in the preheated oven and cook for 15 minutes or until cooked through and golden brown. Mix together the dressing ingredients, season to taste, and serve with the fish.

Haddock with
Green Curry Sauce

2 Servings

225ml coconut cream (see
  right)
pinch of salt
1 tablespoon Green Curry
  Paste (see below)
½ tablespoon palm sugar
2 haddock fillets, each
  weighing about 150g
5 kaffir lime leaves, finely
  sliced
1 large fresh red chilli, sliced
  into thin ovals

Gently heat the coconut cream in a large frying pan, add the salt and stir in the Green Curry Paste, mixing well. Add the palm sugar, stirring constantly. Add the haddock and kaffir lime leaves, then bring slowly to simmering point.

Reduce the heat, cover and poach the fish for 10–15 minutes, depending on its thickness. Transfer the fish to warmed plates, garnish with chillies and serve.

Coconut cream

For this recipe, it is assumed you will use canned coconut milk. If the recipe requires coconut cream, open the tin without shaking it, and separate the thicker white cream from the transparent liquid, scooping it out with a ladle.

Green Curry Paste

Makes roughly 20 tablespoons

100g (roughly 50–60) small
  fresh green chillies
1 teaspoon sea salt
70g shallots, peeled and
  finely chopped
80g garlic, peeled and finely
  chopped
3 tablespoons finely chopped
  galangal
4 lemongrass stalks, finely
  chopped
1 tablespoon finely chopped
  kaffir lime peel
1 teaspoon finely chopped
  coriander root
2 tablespoons white
  peppercorns
1 tablespoon cumin seeds,
  dry-fried
1 tablespoon shrimp paste

The ingredients should be ground using a pestle and mortar. Start with the hardest ingredients then add the other ingredients one at a time. I usually start with the chillies and sea-salt – the coarse salt helps to cut through the chilli skin. As you add each ingredient, check the aroma of the paste to see how the new ingredient is balancing with the previous ones. This will ensure that you don't add too much or too little of any ingredient. You are aiming for a harmonious blend with no one flavour dominating.

Vegetarian
Dishes

Griddled Radicchio & Strawberry Risotto

The bitterness of the radicchio works really well with the sweetness of the strawberries. The recipe is best served with some reduced balsamic vinegar.

2 Servings

For the radicchio:
1 head radicchio,
   approximately 350g
olive oil, for drizzling
sea salt
balsamic vinegar
   (approximately 1
   tablespoon)

For the risotto:
1 tablespoon olive oil
25g butter
2 shallots, finely diced
185g risotto rice (such as
   Arborio or Carnaroli)
150ml white wine
450ml hot vegetable stock
juice of ½ a lemon
2 tablespoons mascarpone
sea salt and pepper
25g Parmesan cheese,
   grated
8 strawberries, quartered
½ tablespoon finely chopped
   chives (optional)

Preheat a griddle pan over a medium heat. Cut the radicchio into quarters lengthways, keeping some of the stem attached to each quarter (trim off any dark parts of the stem). Open the leaves a little, drizzle with olive oil and season with salt. Place the oiled radicchio on the hot griddle and cook for 2–3 minutes on either side. When it begins to brown, remove to a plate and drizzle with a little balsamic vinegar. Leave to cool before shredding it into thin strips.

To make the risotto, heat the olive oil and butter in a heavy-based saucepan over a medium heat, add the shallots and cook until translucent. Add the rice and fry for 1 minute, stirring to prevent it from sticking. Reduce the heat a little and add the wine. Allow the wine to be absorbed before adding a ladle of hot stock (that's approximately 200ml, depending on the size of your ladle). Stir and allow the rice to absorb the stock before adding the next 200ml. Continue to add stock in this way, stirring frequently, until it has all been absorbed and the rice is al dente (with just a bite to it). This will take about 20 minutes. Stir through the lemon juice, radicchio, mascarpone and salt and pepper to taste. Turn off the heat, stir in the Parmesan and half the strawberries.

Serve, garnished with the remaining strawberries, chives, a drizzle of olive oil and reduced balsamic vinegar (see below) or an aged balsamic (optional).

Tip: To make reduced balsamic vinegar, pour a bottle of balsamic vinegar into a small saucepan and warm over a low heat (don't use an expensive balsamic for this). Continue to heat until the balsamic has reduced and coats the back of a spoon. Turn off the heat and pour into a container. Leave to cool before covering; there is no need to refrigerate. If it thickens too much, gently warm in a microwave or in a bowl of boiling water for 5 seconds.

Five-a-Day Mixed Vegetable Stir-Fry

You can vary the vegetables using whatever you have in your fridge. The key to a good stir-fry is to ensure you don't overcook the vegetables by leaving them in the wok or pan too long, and you don't need a lot of oil. For tougher vegetables such as broccoli, you could add a sprinkle of water to help with the cooking process. As a general rule, always add the crunchier vegetables to the wok first and softer ones last – that way all the vegetables still retain their 'bite'.

2 Servings

2 tablespoons groundnut oil
2 garlic cloves, crushed and
   finely chopped
1 tablespoon freshly grated
   ginger
5 dried Chinese mushrooms,
   soaked in hot water for
   20 minutes, finely chopped,
   stem discarded
1 carrot, sliced
1 red pepper, sliced
100g fresh baby corn,
   chopped into 1.5cm pieces
100g mangetout
100g cashew nuts
50ml vegetable stock
1 tablespoon oyster sauce
1 tablespoon light soy sauce
a dash of sesame oil
1 tablespoon cornflour
   blended with 2 tablespoons
   cold water (optional)
1 spring onion, diagonally
   sliced

Heat a wok over a high heat and add the oil. Throw in the garlic and ginger. Cook for less than 1 minute then add the vegetables. Stir-fry for less than 1 minute. Add the cashew nuts and stir-fry for a further minute.

Add the vegetable stock, oyster sauce, light soy sauce and sesame oil.

Stir in the blended cornflour if you prefer a thicker sauce. Throw in the spring onion, give a final stir and then serve immediately with noodles or steamed rice.

Stir-fried Fresh Beancurd, Pak Choy & Oyster Mushrooms in Black Bean Sauce

There are many different varieties of beancurd. It can be fresh, fried, fermented or smoked and is available in soft and firm varieties. The more acidic tofu is more silken in texture. Tofu is extremely nutritious and a good source of low-fat protein because it is made from the milky liquid of crushed soya beans which are pressed and formed to make this cheese-like ingredient.

2 Servings

1 tablespoon vegetable oil
60g oyster mushrooms
200g pak choy leaves, separated
200g fresh tofu, cut into 2cm cubes
200ml hot vegetable stock
1 tablespoon cornflour blended with 2 tablespoons cold water (optional)
fresh sprigs of coriander

For the black bean sauce:
1 tablespoon fermented, salted black beans
2 tablespoons light soy sauce
1 tablespoon shaoxing rice wine or dry sherry
2 garlic cloves, crushed and finely chopped
1 red chilli, deseeded and finely chopped

Blitz all the sauce ingredients in a food-processor but do not process to a smooth sauce – you want to keep some texture to the sauce ingredients.

Heat the wok over high heat and add the oil. Throw in the mushrooms, pak choy and fresh tofu and stir-fry for less than 1 minute.

Add the sauce and stir gently, taking care not to break up the delicate tofu.

Add the stock to the wok and bring to the boil. For a thicker sauce, add the blended cornflour and stir well.

Transfer to a large serving plate, garnish with fresh coriander and serve with steamed rice.

Southern Vegetable Curry

This curry paste is particular to this dish. It doesn't use many ingredients and is quick to make. White peppercorns have a milder taste than black ones.

2 Servings   **GF** Gluten-free   **V** Vegan

450ml water
55g courgettes, cut into
   2.5cm cubes
55g pumpkin, cut into
   2.5cm cubes
55g baby sweetcorn, sliced
   diagonally in half
55g oyster mushrooms,
   separated
1 medium tomato, quartered
10 sweet basil leaves

For the curry paste:
¼ teaspoon white
   peppercorns
2 small dried red chillies
¼ teaspoon salt
3 small Thai shallots

First make the curry paste. Pound the peppercorns in a stone mortar to a powder, then add the chillies and pound again. Add the salt and shallots and pound the mixture into a paste.

Bring the water to the boil in a pan and stir in the curry paste. Add the vegetables, reduce the heat and simmer for 20 minutes, stirring occasionally. Add the basil leaves and serve.

Capri Lemon Pasta with Peas, Broad Beans & Asparagus

This is such a simple dish, yet perfectly balanced and bursting with flavour. The vegetables added here can be varied (courgettes – green and yellow – would work as well as their flowers).

 2 Servings

150ml double cream
juice and finely grated zest of
   1 lemon
a small bunch of asparagus
225g fresh broad beans,
   podded (or 80g frozen)
200g fresh pasta (such
   as linguine, tagliatelle or
   spaghetti)
225g fresh peas, podded (or
   80g frozen)
2 tablespoons mascarpone
40g Parmesan cheese,
   grated
a small bunch of basil, torn
salt and freshly ground black
   pepper

Put a large pot of salted water on to the boil. Meanwhile, pour the cream and lemon zest into a saucepan and carefully bring to the boil, then simmer for 3 minutes.

While the cream is simmering, prepare the asparagus: snap off the woody ends and cut into 3cm pieces. You could also peel the outer skin from the broad beans.

Cook the pasta, peas, broad beans and asparagus together in the boiling water for 3 minutes or until the pasta is al dente. Reserve 50ml of cooking water and drain the pasta, peas, beans and asparagus.

Pour the cream into the cooking pot, add the lemon juice, mascarpone and reserved cooking water. Return to the boil, add the pasta and vegetables, Parmesan, basil and seasoning and toss together. Divide between 2 bowls and serve immediately.

Leek
& Potato Soup

This vibrant, warming soup makes a satisfying lunch on a chilly day.

 2 Servings **GF** Gluten-free

a glug of vegetable oil
2 small potatoes, cut into
  1cm cubes
½ leek, sliced into 5mm
  rounds, and well rinsed
375ml gluten-free vegetable
  stock
100ml semi-skimmed milk or
  soya milk
salt and freshly ground black
  pepper

Heat the oil in a saucepan over a medium heat, stir in the vegetables and cook for 2 minutes.

Add the vegetable stock and bring to the boil over a high heat. When it is boiling reduce the heat and simmer for 20 minutes.

When the vegetables are cooked take the saucepan off the heat. With a ladle carefully put 3 ladlefuls of the soup in a blender and blend for 10 seconds. Then pour the blended soup into a big bowl.

Repeat the blending until the saucepan is empty. Pour the blended soup back into the saucepan and reheat gently.

Add the milk, salt and pepper and simmer for 2 minutes more, then serve.

Carrot Batons with Pine Kernals

Tender carrots and toasted pine kernels make for a great vegetarian side dish.

2 Servings

1 tablespoon olive oil
½ small onion, finely
   chopped
a handful of pine kernels
350g carrot batons
100ml chicken stock
1 tablespoon fresh parsley,
   finely chopped
a drizzle virgin olive oil
salt and freshly ground black
   pepper

Heat the oil in a saucepan over a moderate heat and fry the onion gently for 2–3 minutes. Add the pine kernals and cook for a further minute, then add the carrots and chicken stock and season to taste.

Cover and cook gently for 5–10 minutes until the carrots are tender. Toss the parsley through the carrots and serve in a warm bowl with a drizzle of olive oil.

Fresh Baked Aubergines & Peppers

A versatile dish that can be served as an accompaniment to meat or fish, or added to pasta to make a tasty vegetarian main course.

 **2** Servings **GF** Gluten-free **V** Vegan

65ml olive oil

1 medium aubergine, sliced lengthways into 1cm thick slices

1 red pepper, deseeded and cut into quarters

10g thyme, leaves removed from the stems

salt and freshly ground black pepper

15g pine kernels

15g sultanas

Preheat the oven to 200°C/400°F/gas mark 6.

Using a tablespoon of the olive oil, lightly oil a large baking sheet, then place the aubergine slices and peppers on a tray in a single layer.

Brush liberally with the remaining olive oil, then sprinkle with thyme and season with salt and freshly ground black pepper. Bake in the oven for 15–20 minutes, adding the pine kernels and sultanas a couple of minutes before the cooking time is complete. Serve immediately.

Variations: Cook wedges of red onion with the aubergines and peppers for a touch of added sweetness.

Toss the vegetables with cooked pasta and add cubes of mozzarella or feta cheese for a delicious vegetarian supper.

INDEX

apple, caramelised, spiced lentils
and duck breast 60–1
artichoke and tomato warm salad,
with lamb cutlets 66–7
asparagus, peas, broad beans
and capri lemon pasta 112–13
aubergine, fruity baked, with
peppers 118–19

bacon
cabbage and crispy onions
44–5
and egg-fried rice 32–3
sherry vinegar and
pan-fried scallops 78–9
bamboo shoots and curried fish
balls 83
basil and orange stuffing with red
mullet 96–7
beancurd, stir-fried fresh, pak
choy and oyster mushrooms in
black bean sauce 108–9
beans
broad, asparagus, peas and
capri lemon pasta 112–13
and pan-fried pork 50–1
white, truffle puree 28–9
beef
Burmese-style curry, with
vermicelli rice noodles 56–7
Sichuan pepper, five-a-day
vegetables and five-spice
gravy 52–3
Wellington, with mushroom
and mustard sauce 64–5
bergamot sauce and pork fillets
68–9
blue cheese, rosemary and
caramelised onion pizza 38–9
broad beans, asparagus, peas
and capri lemon pasta 112–13
broccoli, mozzarella and garlic
sliver pizza 40–1
butter, maitre d'hotel 84

cabbage, crispy onions and
bacon 44–5
carrot
batons, with prosciutto 116–17
five-a-day mixed vegetable
stir-fry 106–7
cavolo nero and pancetta
pappardelle 26–7
chicken
caramelised 48–9
warm smoked, red onion
and spinach salad 20–1
and winter tarragon parcel
70–1
chickpea
and feta salad, with peppers
and coriander 14–15
salt cod, roasted red onion
and parsley salad 18–19
chilli prawns, hot, on yellow shi
noodles 30–1
Chinese mushroom, five-a-day
mixed vegetable stir-fry 106–7
clam(s), pasta with 88–9
cod
Parmesan-crusted, with
tomato and olive dressing
98–9
see also salt cod
compote, gooseberries 76–7
courgette, southern vegetable
curry 110–11
crab and mushroom quick
kedgeree 94–5
cucumber, tzatziki 58–9
curry
Burmese-style beef, with
vermicelli rice noodles 56–7
curried fish balls and
bamboo shoots 82–3
green paste 101
green sauce, with haddock
100–1

jungle curry paste 83
paste 111
southern vegetable 110–11

duck breast, spiced lentils and
caramelised apples 60–1

egg(s)
fried rice and bacon 32–3
spicy Indian omelette 34–5
see also quail's egg(s)
elderflower, gooseberries and
grilled mackerel 76–7
endive, pear, pancetta and
toasted pinenut salad 12–13

fennel
grapefruit, caper and
parsley salad with pan-fried
mackerel 80–1
lemon and fusilli tricolore 42–3
feta and chickpea salad with
peppers and coriander 14–15
fish balls, curried, and bamboo
shoots 82–3
fusilli tricolore, lemon and fennel
42–3

garlic sliver, broccoli and
mozzarella pizza 40–1
gooseberry
compote 76–7
elderflower and grilled
mackerel 76–7
grapefruit, caper, parsley and
fennel salad with pan-fried
mackerel 80–1
gravy, five-spice, five-a-day
vegetables and Sichuan pepper
beef 52–3

haddock with green curry sauce
100–1
ham, smoked, and mushroom

Recipe Acknowledgements

We would like to thank the following authors for kind permission to reproduce their recipes:

Chapter 1: Salads
p.13 Pear, Pancetta, Toasted Pinenut & Endive Salad from *Easy Peasy* by Sophie Wright
p.14 Feta & Chickpea Salad with Peppers & Coriander from *Stylish Mediterranean in Minutes* by Sophie Braimbridge
p.17 Cos Lettuce, Tuna, Quail's Eggs & Roasted Plum Tomatoes from *Fast & Fresh* by Oded Schwartz and Maddalena Bonino
p.18 Chickpea, Salt Cod, Roasted Red Onion & Parsley Salad from *Fast & Fresh* by Oded Schwartz and Maddalena Bonino
p.21 Warm Smoked Chicken, Red Onion & Spinach Salad from *Fast & Fresh* by Oded Schwartz and Maddalena Bonino

Chapter 2: Light Meals
p.24 Smoked Ham & Mushroom Risotto from *The Gluten-free Cookbook* edited by Kyle Cathie
p.27 Pappardelle with Pancetta & Cavolo Nero from *Easy Italian in Minutes* edited by Kyle Cathie
p.28 Rosemary Porcini from *The Modern Vegetarian* by Maria Elia
p.31 Hot Chilli Prawns on Yellow Shi Noodles from *China Modern* by Ching-He Huang
p.32 Bacon & Egg-fried Rice from *China Modern* by Ching-He Huang
p.35 Spicy Indian Omelette from *Ballymaloe Cookery Course* by Darina Allen
p.36 Cheat's Margherita Pizza from *Easy Italian in Minutes* edited by Kyle Cathie
pp.38-9 Pizza with Caramelised Onions, Blue Cheese & Rosemary from *Ballymaloe Cookery Course* by Darina Allen
p.40 Pizza with Broccoli, Mozzarella & Garlic Slivers from *Ballymaloe Cookery Course* by Darina Allen
p.43 Fusilli Tricolore with Lemon & Fennel from *Easy Italian in Minutes* edited by Kyle Cathie
p.44 Bacon & Cabbage with Crispy Onions from *Classic British Cookbook* edited by Kyle Cathie

Chapter 3: Meat Dishes
p.48 Caramelised Chicken from *Home at 7, Dinner at 8* by Sophie Wright
p.51 Pan-fried Pork with Beans from *Easy Italian in Minutes* edited by Kyle Cathie
p.53 Sichuan Pepper Beef with Five-a-day Vegetables & Five-spice Gravy from *China Modern* by Ching-He Huang
p.55 Pigeon with Pomegranate Sauce from *Stylish Mediterranean in Minutes* by Sophie Braimbridge
p.56 Burmese-style Beef Curry with Vermicelli Rice Noodles from *China Modern* by

Ching-He Huang

p.59 Lamb Kebabs with Tzatziki from *Ballymaloe Cookery Course* by
Darina Allen

p.61 Duck Breast with Spiced Lentils & Caramelised Apples from *Ballymaloe Cookery Course* by Darina Allen

p.62 Pork Tenderloin with Pears & Sweet Sherry from *Stylish Mediterranean in Minutes* by
Sophie Braimbridge

p.65 Beef Wellington with Mushroom & Mustard Sauce from *Classic British Cookbook* edited
by Kyle Cathie

p.66 Lamb Cutlets on a Warm Tomato & Artichoke Salad from *Fast & Fresh* by Oded
Schwartz and Maddalena Bonino

p.69 Pork Fillets with Bergamot Sauce from *Jekka's Herb Book* by Jekka McVicar

p.70 Chicken & Winter Tarragon Parcel from *Jekka's Herb Book* by Jekka McVicar

p.73 Pheasant Braised with Cork Gin from *Forgotten Skills of Cooking* by Darina Allen

Chapter 4: Fish & Seafood

p.76 Grilled Mackerel with Gooseberries & Elderflower from *Scandinavian Kitchen* by
Camilla Plum

p.79 Pan-fried Scallops with Bacon & Sherry Vinegar from *Stylish Mediterranean in Minutes*
by Sophie Braimbridge

p.80 Pan-fried Mackerel with Fennel, Grapefruit, Caper & Parsley Salad from *Easy Peasy* by
Sophie Wright

p.83 Curried Fish Balls with Bamboo Shoots from *The Big Book of Thai Curries* by Vatcharin
Bhumichitr

p.84 Proper Breakfast Kippers from *Forgotten Skills of Cooking* by Darina Allen

p.87 Scallops on Pea Purée from *Classic British Cookbook* edited by Kyle Cathie

p.88 Pasta with Clams from *Stylish Mediterranean in Minutes* by Sophie Braimbridge

p.91 Roast Salmon with Watercress Sauce from *Classic British Cookbook* edited by
Kyle Cathie

p.92 Roasted John Dory with Roasted Tomato & Olive Salsa from *Fast & Fresh* by Oded
Schwartz and Maddalena Bonino

p.95 Quick Crab & Mushroom Kedgeree from *Seriously Good! Gluten-free Cooking* by
Phil Vickery

p.96 Baked Red Mullet with Vine Leaves from *Stylish Mediterranean in Minutes* by
Sophie Braimbridge

p.99 Parmesan-crusted Cod with Tomato & Olive Dressing from *Easy Italian in Minutes*
edited by Kyle Cathie

p.101 Haddock with Green Curry Sauce from *The Big Book of Thai Curries* by Vatcharin
Bhumichitr

Chapter 5: Vegetarian Dishes

p.104 Griddled Radicchio & Strawberry Risotto from *The Modern Vegetarian* by Maria Elia

p.107 Five-a-Day Mixed Vegetable Stir-Fry from *China Modern* by Ching-He Huang

p.108 Stir-fried Fresh Beancurd, Pak Choy & Oyster Mushrooms in Black Bean Sauce from *China Modern* by Ching-He Huang

p.111 Southern Vegetable Curry from *The Big Book of Thai Curries* by Vatcharin Bhumichitr

p.112 Capri Lemon Pasta with Peas Broad Beans & Asparagus by *The Modern Vegetarian* by Maria Elia

p.115 Leek & Potato Soup from *The Gluten-free Cookbook* edited by Kyle Cathie

p.116 Carrot Batons with Pine Kernels from *Easy Italian in Minutes* edited by Kyle Cathie

p.119 Fresh Baked Aubergines and Peppers from *Easy Italian in Minutes* edited by Kyle Cathie

Photography Acknowledgements

We would like to thank the following photographers for kind permission to reproduce their images:

p.2, pp.4–5, p.6 William Reavell
p.7 Kate Whitaker from *China Modern* by Ching-He Huang
p.9 Gus Filgate from *Easy Italian in Minutes* edited by Kyle Cathie

Chapter 1: Salads
p.12 Kate Whitaker from *Easy Peasy* by Sophie Wright
p.15 Mano Chatzikonstantis from *Stylish Mediterranean in Minutes* by Sophie Braimbridge
p.16, p.19, p.20 William Reavell

Chapter 2: Light Meals
p.25 Gus Filgate from *The Gluten-free Cookbook* edited by Kyle Cathie
p.26 Gus Filgate from *Easy Italian in Minutes* edited by Kyle Cathie
p.29 Jonathan Gregson from *The Modern Vegetarian* by Maria Elia
p.30, p.32 Kate Whitaker from *China Modern* by Ching-He Huang
p.35 William Reavell
p.37 Gus Filgate from *Easy Italian in Minutes* edited by Kyle Cathie
p.39, p.41 William Reavell
p.42 Gus Filgate from *Easy Italian in Minutes* edited by Kyle Cathie
p.44 Gus Filgate from *Classic British Cookbook* edited by Kyle Cathie

Chapter 3: Meat Dishes
p.49 Romas Foord from *Home at 7, Dinner at 8* by Sophie Wright
p.50 Gus Filgate from *Easy Italian in Minutes* edited by Kyle Cathie
p.52 Kate Whitaker from *China Modern* by Ching-He Huang
p.54 Mano Chatzikonstantis from *Stylish Mediterranean in Minutes* by Sophie Braimbridge
p.57 Kate Whitaker from *China Modern* by Ching-He Huang
p.58, p.60 Ray Main from *Darina Allen's Ballymaloe Cookery Course* by Darina Allen
p.62 Mano Chatzikonstantis from *Stylish Mediterranean in Minutes* by Sophie Braimbridge
p.64 Gus Filgate from *Classic British Cookbook* edited by Kyle Cathie
p.67 William Reavell
p.68, p.71 Jekka McVicar from *Jekka's Herb Book* by Jekka McVicar
p.72 Peter Cassidy from *Forgotten Skills of Cooking* by Darina Allen

Chapter 4: Fish & Seafood

p.77 Anne-Li Engström from *Scandinavian Kitchen* by Camilla Plum

p.78 Mano Chatzikonstantis from *Stylish Mediterranean in Minutes* by Sophie Braimbridge

p.81 Kate Whitaker from *Easy Peasy* by Sophie Wright

p.82 Martin Brigdale from *The Big Book of Thai Curries* by Vatcharin Bhumichitr

p.85 Peter Cassidy from *Forgotten Skills of Cooking* by Darina Allen

p.86 Gus Filgate from *Classic British Cookbook* edited by Kyle Cathie

p.89 Mano Chatzikonstantis from *Stylish Mediterranean in Minutes* by Sophie Braimbridge

p.90 Gus Filgate from *Classic British Cookbook* edited by Kyle Cathie

p.92 William Reavell

p.94 Steve Lee from *Seriously Good! Gluten-free Cooking* by Phil Vickery

p.97 Mano Chatzikonstantis from *Stylish Mediterranean in Minutes* by Sophie Braimbridge

p.98 Gus Filgate from *Easy Italian in Minutes* edited by Kyle Cathie

p.100 Martin Brigdale from *The Big Book of Thai Curries* by Vatcharin Bhumichitr

Chapter 5: Vegetarian Dishes

p.105 Jonathan Gregson from *The Modern Vegetarian* by Maria Elia

p.106, p.109 Kate Whitaker from *China Modern* by Ching-He Huang

p.110 Martin Brigdale from *The Big Book of Thai Curries* by Vatcharin Bhumichitr

p.113 Jonathan Gregson by *The Modern Vegetarian* by Maria Elia

p.114 Gus Filgate from *The Gluten-free Cookbook* edited by Kyle Cathie

p.117, p.118 Gus Filgate from *Easy Italian in Minutes* edited by Kyle Cathie

p.128 William Reavell